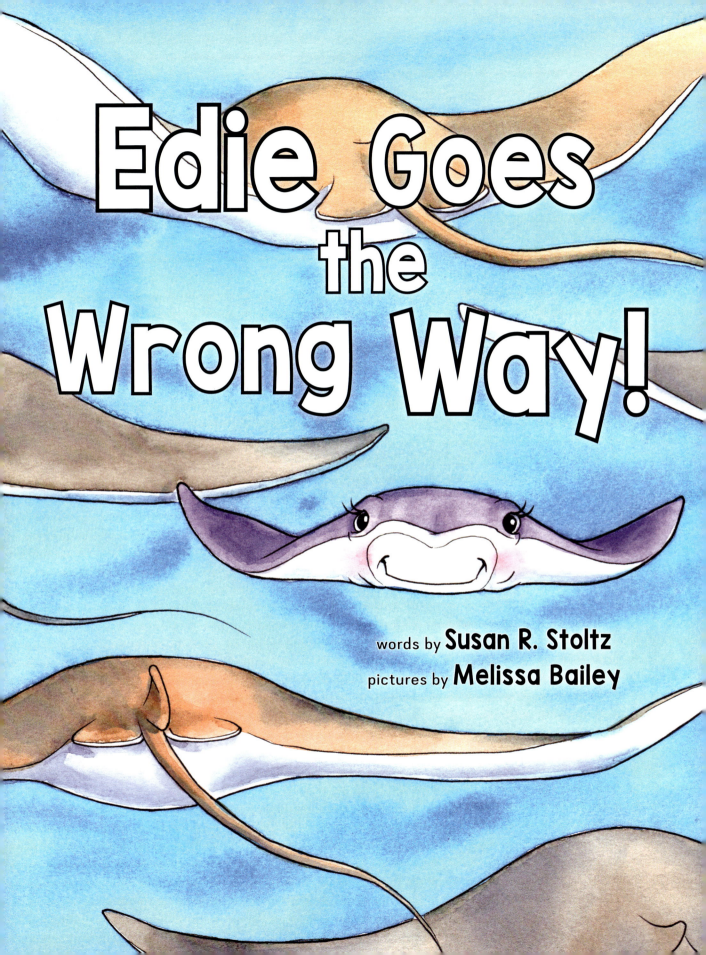

For my granddaughter Amelia.
You are loved.

Pygmy Giraffe Publishing, Douglas, Wyoming 82633

Copyright © 2018 by Susan R. Stoltz

All Rights Reserved.
No part of this publication may be produced in any form or
by any means without written permission of Pygmy Giraffe Publishing
except for the use of brief quotations in a book review.

ISBN-13: 978-0-578-42139-1
ISBN-10: 0-578-42139-9

Pygmy Giraffe Publishing is committed to providing products
that are safe for our children and our planet.
Printed on sustainably-sourced paper with earth-friendly soy ink.
Printed in the United States of America

About This Book

All the animals featured in this book are real fish that live in the sea, however they don't actually have picnics or play musical instruments under the water. That part is make-believe for this story. Wouldn't it be interesting to study about them? For instance, the surgeon fish is also called a blue tang. Is it endangered? No. But others in this book are endangered, such as some kinds of sharks, seahorses, and sawfish. Endangered means there aren't very many of them left in the world.

So, have some fun! Do a little research about endangered fish and discover other amazing facts about the beautiful animals that live in our oceans.

Edie was a tiny ray
Who swam around all day,
And didn't seem to understand
She was going the wrong way!

Sometimes her wrong-way swimming style
Confused the other fish.
To see things very differently
Was Edie's greatest wish.

"Why don't you swim like all of us?"
Complained the other rays.
"I want to do exciting things!"
She would always say.

"To see the sun from over here
And find the sky so blue.
Seaweed growing up like trees,
So green, of different hues."

"Your faces are so fun to see
Instead of just your tails.
And tell me, please, was there a time
You chatted with a whale?"

"I'd like to see an octopus.
Do lion fishes roar?
Does a swordfish use his pointy nose
To roast marshmallows for s'mores?"

"Do sawfishes and hammerheads
Build houses just for fun?
Have you ever gathered grains of sand
And stacked them one by one?"

"Your questions make us think you're nuts!"
The other rays declared.
"Please turn around and swim our way.
You're giving us a scare."

Little Edie tried her best
To be like all her friends.
She turned and swam like all the rest
And tried hard to pretend.

Unhappy, Edie moped and sulked
And dreamed of such a time
When she could ask a jellyfish
If on toast it was divine.

She wanted to explore her world,
New adventures every week.
Questions raced inside her head.
More answers she did seek.

Is the jazzy trumpet fish
A member of a band?
Or does he just blow through his nose
And scatter all the sand?

Does the horseshoe crab make certain
That the seahorse has on shoes?
And does the hairy angelfish
Use conditioning shampoo?

Edie chose to leave her friends.
Sometimes she felt alone,
But mostly she was quite content
Exploring the unknown.

She passed a little surgeon fish
Working on a shark,
Assisted by the forceps crab.
She was having such a lark.

A dandy picnic she once found.
So many fish were there.
A mustard tang and lemon shark
Were starting to prepare...

Sea cucumbers with butterfish.
For dessert? Banana wrasse.
They always asked politely, "Please?"
When yummy food was passed.

One day she swam down very deep.
It was really rather risky.
Adventure seemed to call her name
And she was feeling frisky.

Fathoms deep below the sea
A pirate ship she found.
Dark and scary, on its side
It rested on the ground.

A pirate's bones sat ghostly pale,
A parrot fish on his shoulder.
There was something shiny deep inside.
Edie got a little bolder.

Gold doubloons and oyster pearls
Down in the hull they gleamed.
And sand dollars were littered 'round
So white they seemed to beam.

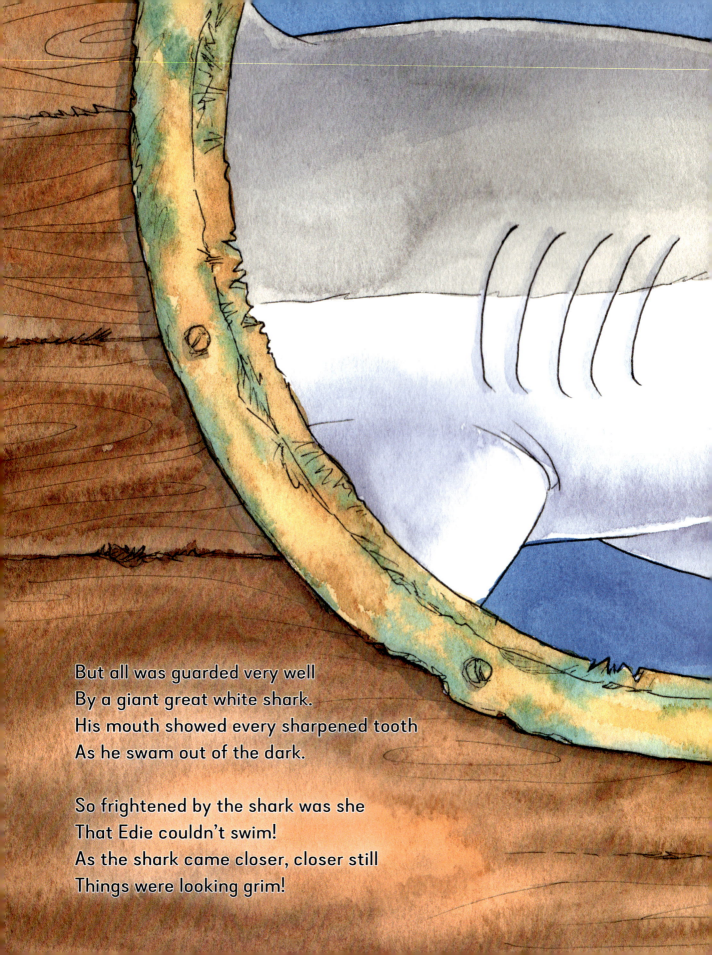

But all was guarded very well
By a giant great white shark.
His mouth showed every sharpened tooth
As he swam out of the dark.

So frightened by the shark was she
That Edie couldn't swim!
As the shark came closer, closer still
Things were looking grim!

Suddenly, with a burst of speed
She overcame her fear.
She took one breath and swam so fast
She seemed to disappear.

Edie swam for years and years,
Made friends along the way.
So many fish accepted her
She knew she was okay.

One day while she was swimming free
She met the other rays.
She had so much to talk about.
She knew they'd be amazed.

The stingrays listened carefully
To the stories she conveyed.
They looked at her in disbelief
At all her escapades.

Her tales distressed the rays so much
That they told her what to do.
"Come home with us and swim our way."
But she quietly withdrew.

Edie had to be herself
Despite the hurtful chatter.
She was good and kind, a thoughtful ray.
And that's what really matters.

She swam the oceans by herself,
Exploring every wave.
Was it wrong for her to swim HER way?
Of course not. It was brave!

About Edie

A female Cownose Stingray named Edie was born at the Phoenix Zoo on November 27, 2013. Her keepers noticed that from the moment she was born, Edie liked to explore and do things her own way. She was curious by nature, preferring to swim in the opposite direction from the other stingrays. Little Edie quickly became a favorite of zoo staff and guests alike. She currently lives in Brownsville, Texas, along with several other stingray pups born at the Phoenix Zoo in the fall of 2013.

About Cownose Stingrays

Cownose Stingrays are fish that live in the ocean. The name Cownose comes from the shape of the head, which looks a lot like . . . you guessed it . . . a cow's nose. They are classified as stingrays because they are born with a barb, sometimes called a stinger, on the base of the tail. The barb is used for defense against a shark attack or anything else they perceive as a threat. The barb is sharp and has venom, which makes it very painful to get stung by a stingray.

Cownose Stingrays are closely related to sharks and can weigh up to 50 pounds. They are peaceful unless you disturb them, and they are also intelligent and curious animals. Their favorite foods include clams, oysters, shrimp, and small fish.

Cownose Stingrays are known to swim long distances, which is called migration. They migrate in large groups, with as many as 10,000 swimming together in one group. Did you know that a group of stingrays is called a fever of rays?

Their numbers are declining in the oceans, mostly due to fishing. But they are not currently considered to be endangered.

Sarah Ekstrom – Former Zookeeper, Phoenix Zoo

Training Stingrays

Stingrays are intelligent and social animals, which makes training them both interesting and rewarding! Stingrays can learn to perform a variety of tasks through simple commands.

Did you know we use underwater hand signals to communicate with stingrays? It's true! They learn to recognize the signals and translate them into the desired response or action we're requesting them to perform. It's extremely important that the training be a positive experience so the stingrays will repeat the behavior when asked. We reward them with tasty food or physical contact for positive reinforcement.

When I work with our stingrays, they learn to perform tasks such as to carry a hoop on their snout, follow targets, and remain stationary in my arms. Pretty cool, right?

Many of the tasks they learn are to help them in case they need medical attention. Imagine how difficult it is to examine a stingray as it swims rapidly under the water! By staying stationary the stingray can participate in its examination with little or no stress.

Training animals is a partnership of trust and respect between those involved. Stingrays are fascinating animals and we've only just begun to learn about their capabilities.

Working with stingrays is such a joy and allows me to discover more each day about these often misunderstood and amazing animals!

Mari Belko – Stingray Keeper, Phoenix Zoo

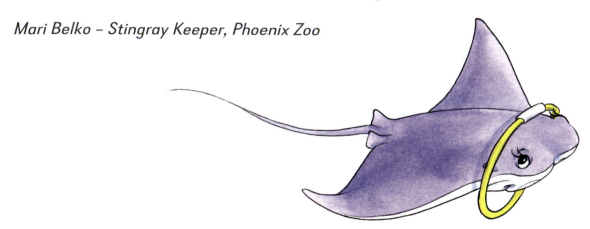

Curriculum is available for *Edie Goes the Wrong Way*. This unit contains eight different lessons to be used in kindergarten through fourth grade classrooms, aligned with National Common Core Literacy Standards.

Please visit www.pygmygiraffepublishing.com for purchase information.